YOUR BABY WILL FIND YOU

A STORY ABOUT LOSS, GRIEF, AND HEALING

Written by
madeleine garner

Illustrated by
giorgia lupi

BenBella

BenBella Books, Inc.
Dallas, TX

BenBella Books, Inc.
10440 N. Central Expressway, Suite 800
Dallas, TX 75231
benbellabooks.com
Send feedback to feedback@benbellabooks.com

BenBella is a federally registered trademark.

Printed in China
10 9 8 7 6 5 4 3 2 1

Library of Congress Control Number: 2024946641
ISBN 9781637746721 (hardcover)
ISBN 9781637746738 (electronic)

Editing by Leah Wilson
Printed by Dream Colour Printing Ltd.

Special discounts for bulk sales are available.
Please contact bulkorders@benbellabooks.com.

*To Brandon, my future, and
to Leila, our baby who found us*

M.G.

To my mom

G.L.

This is you.

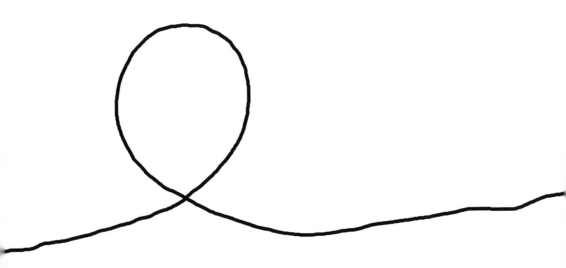

This is you and your baby.

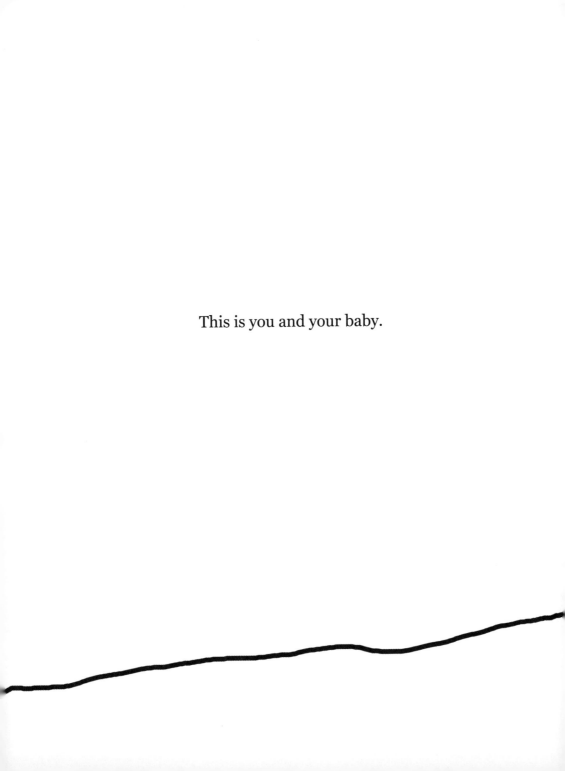

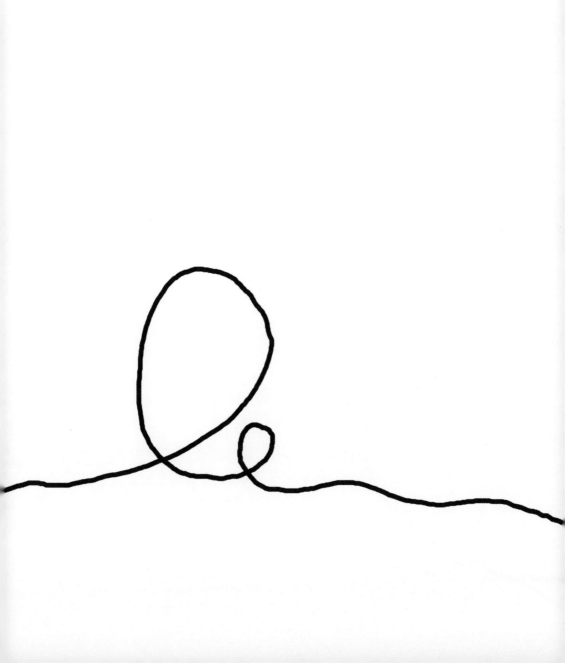

When this was you,
you thought about the
future a lot.

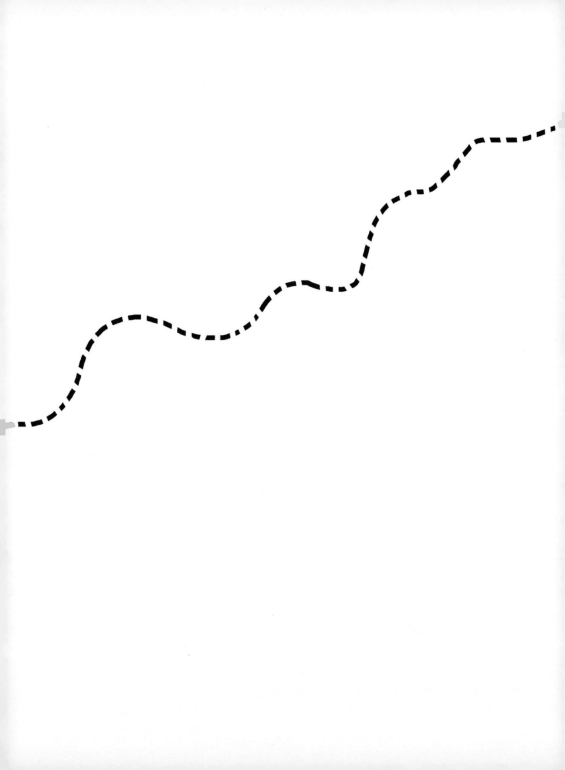

You wondered if you would
be partnered,

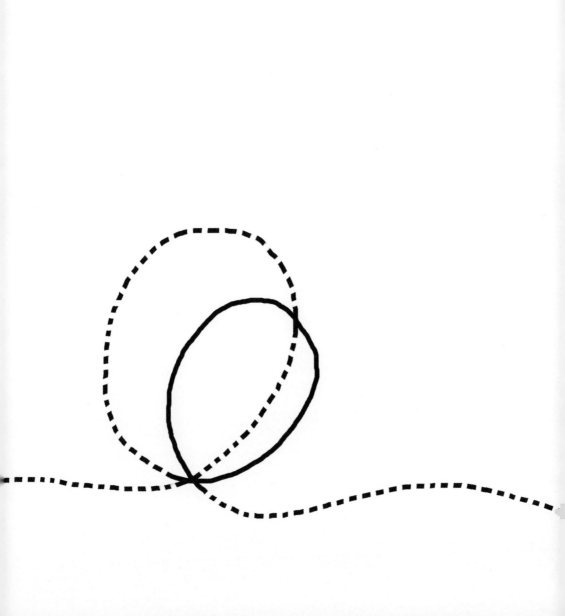

Have a cat,

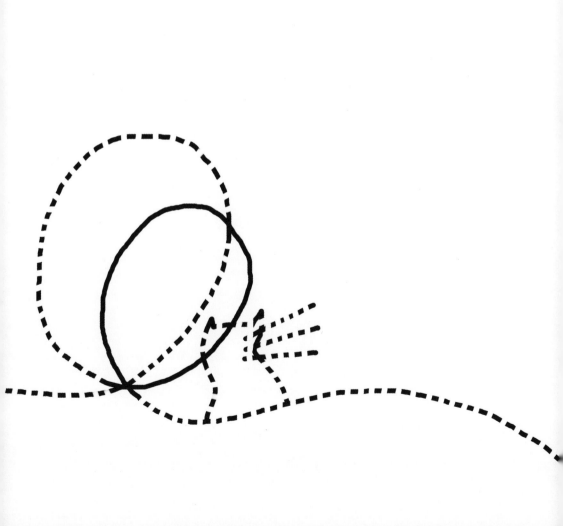

Live in a cozy home.

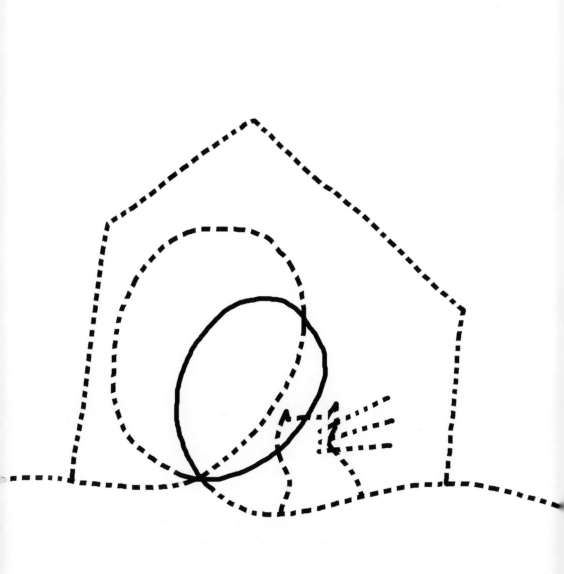

But most of all,
you hoped your future
would include a baby.

You felt destined to be
a mama and hoped your baby
would find you soon.

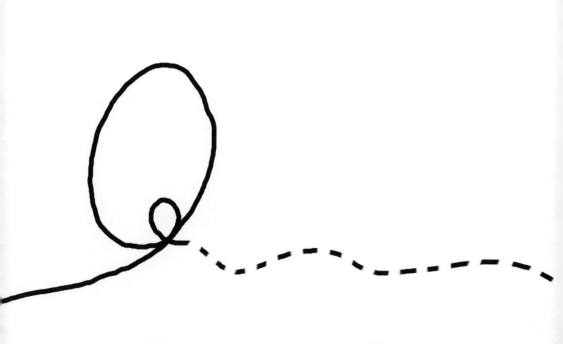

And here you are.

You have a partner, a cat,
and a cozy home.

All set, all ready.

For baby.

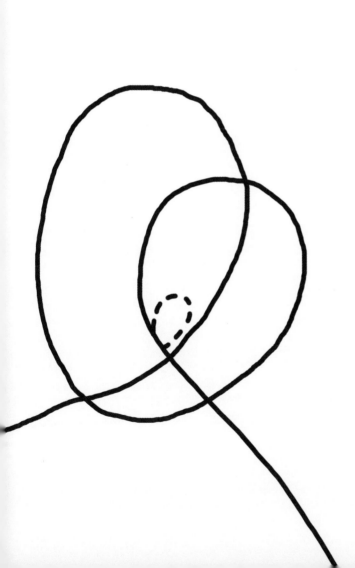

The first month you try by
just seeing what happens.

That doesn't work.

 A

 ∫

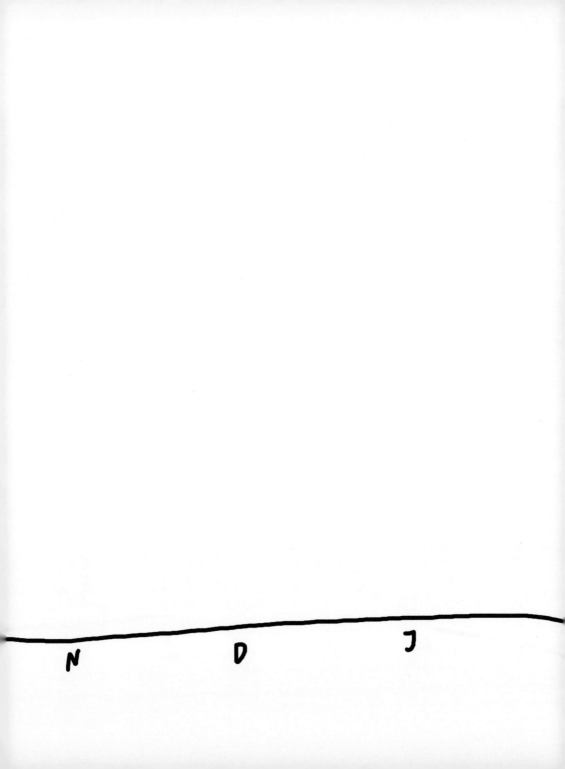

The second month you get
sick halfway through and eat
chicken noodle soup instead.

That doesn't work either.

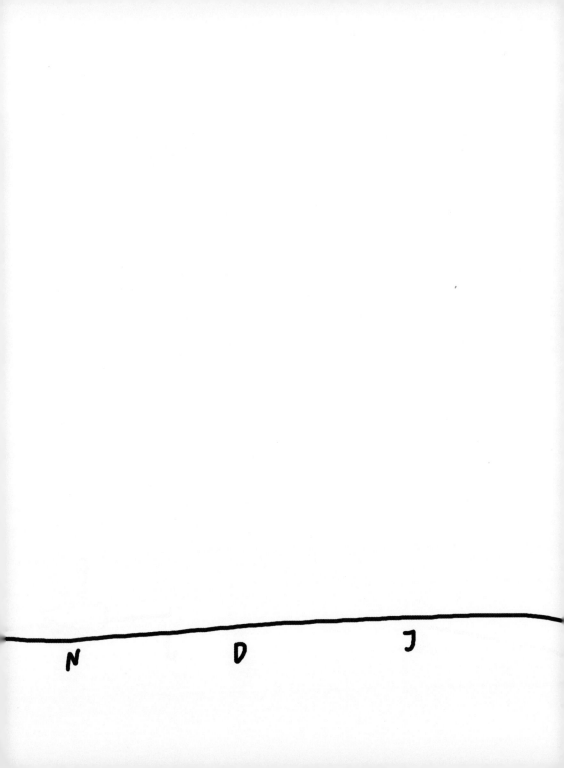

N   D   J

The third month you track
many things, become methodical,
turn trying into a science.

That works!

A   ∫

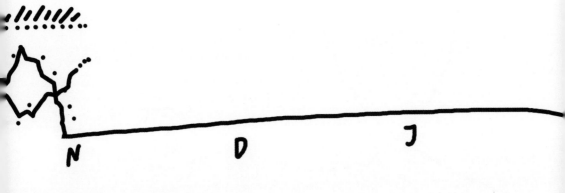

N   D   J

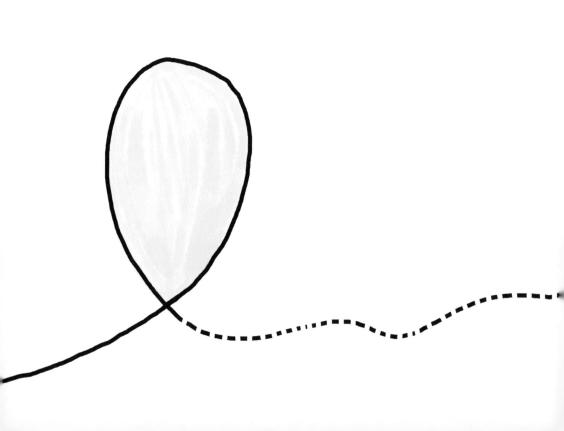

And like magic you
are transformed.

You look the same on the outside,
but on the inside, things have
quickly begun to change.

There is a sesame seed–sized
secret within you working hard
to nestle into place, get comfy,
and prepare for your life together.

You think, your baby
has found you!

The future has arrived.

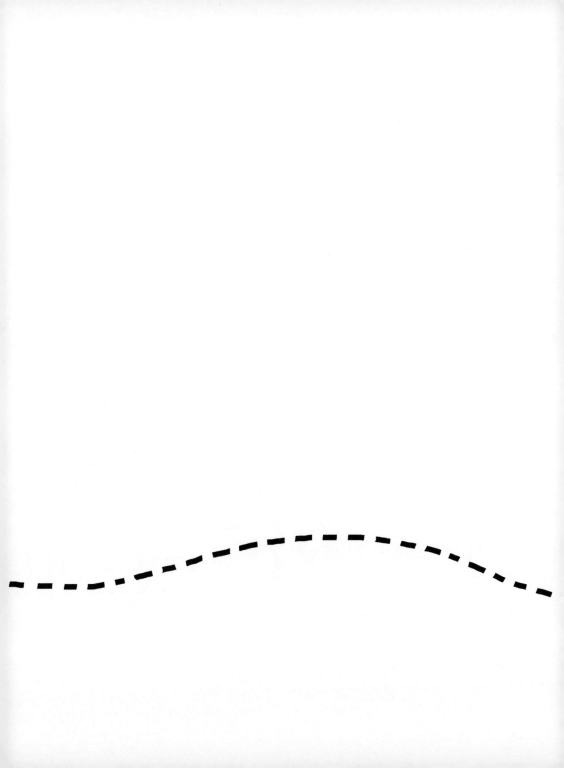

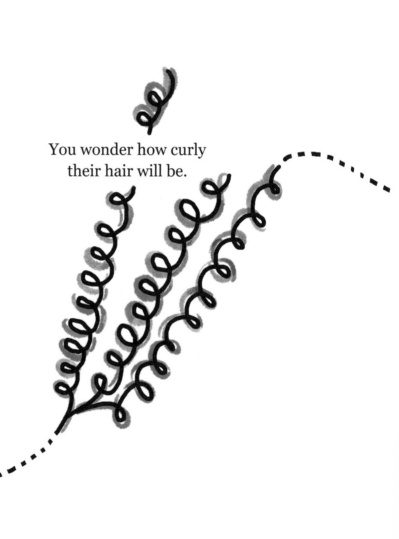

You wonder how curly
their hair will be.

If their eyes will sparkle
when they look up at you.

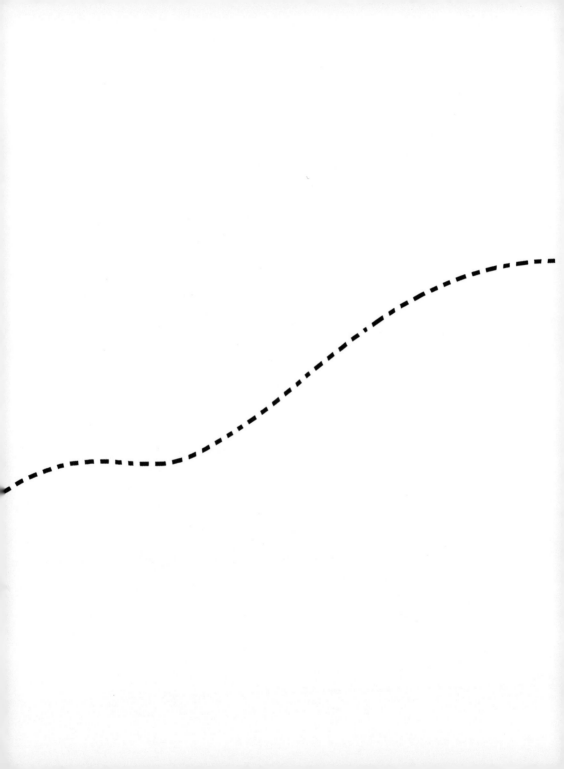

How much they are
going to make you laugh.

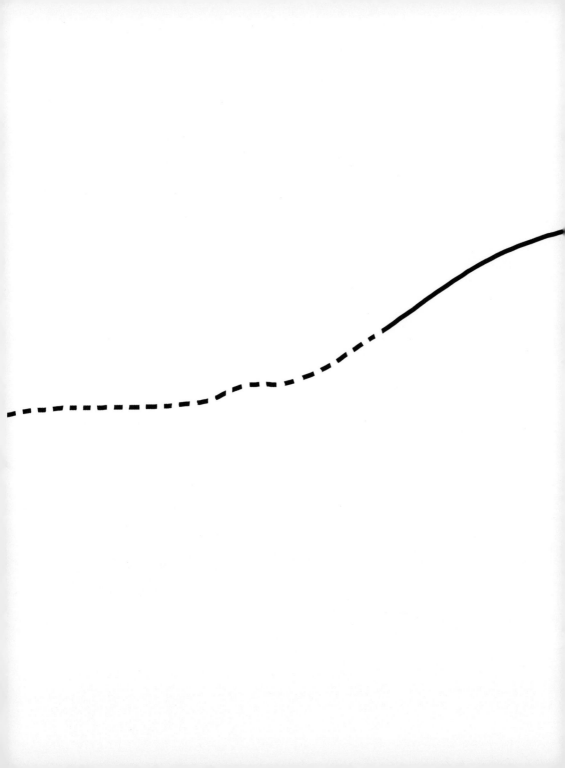

You even envision
that special day when
you will meet them for
the very first time,

And you will tell them
how they came to be.

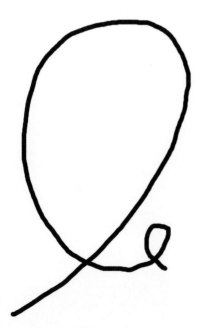

But you are getting
ahead of yourself.

That day is a long way off.

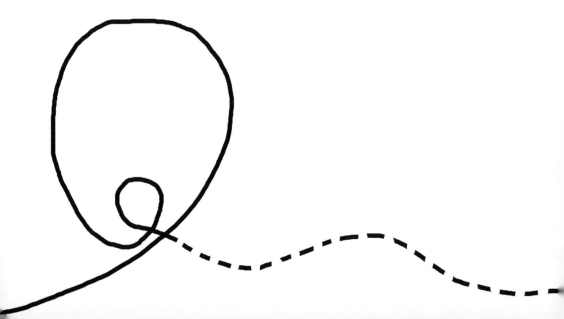

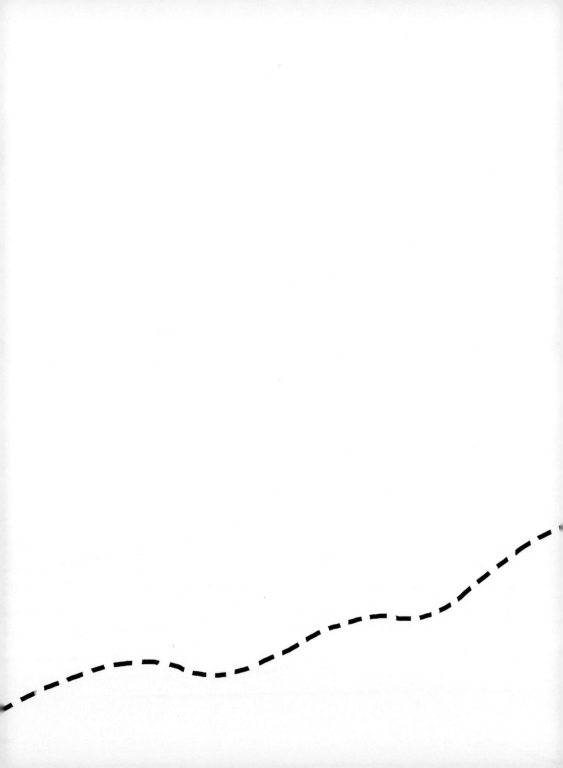

Days pass slowly.

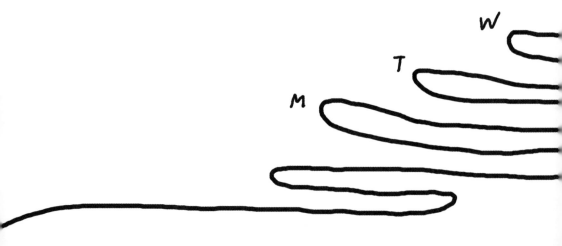

When the sun is out,
you feel peaceful and content.

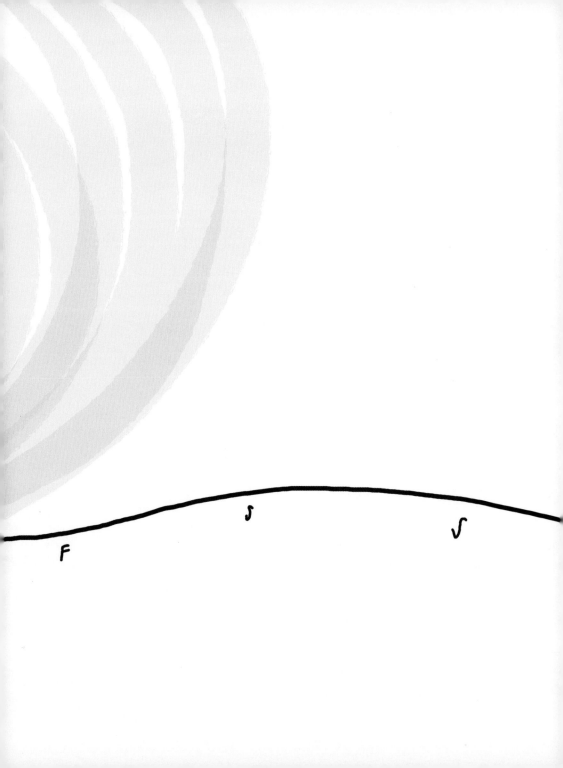

When the sun goes down,
you are full of worry and fear.

This surprises you.

But you can't stop
thinking.

Sometimes things go wrong.

Sometimes futures
are not meant to be.

Your best friend reassures you.

Your dad comforts you.

Your partner calms you.

WHY SHOULD

you ARE

you ARE

≡

HAT BE you?

STRONG and HEALTHY!

READY and PREPARED

≡

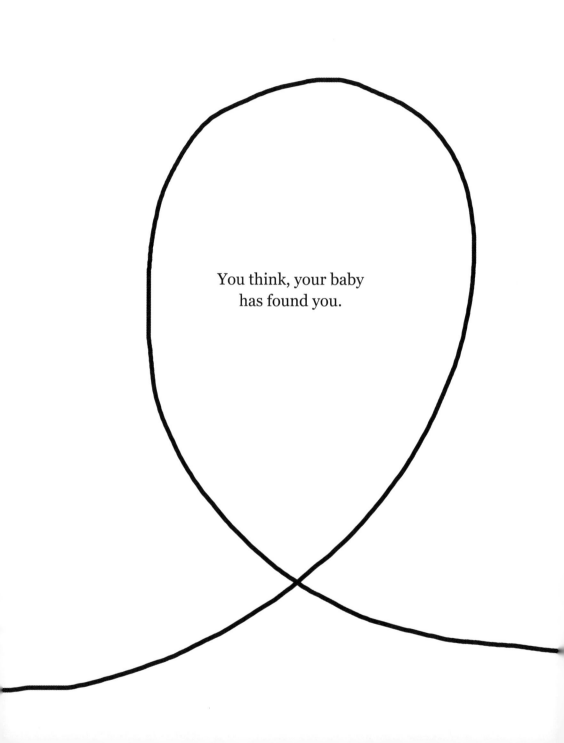

You think, your baby
has found you.

They are sure to
want to stay.

One afternoon in November,
you go to hear your baby's heartbeat
for the first time.

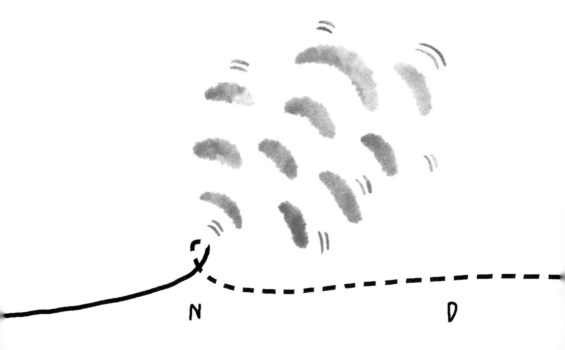

The speedy
thump-thump-thumps
will be like music.

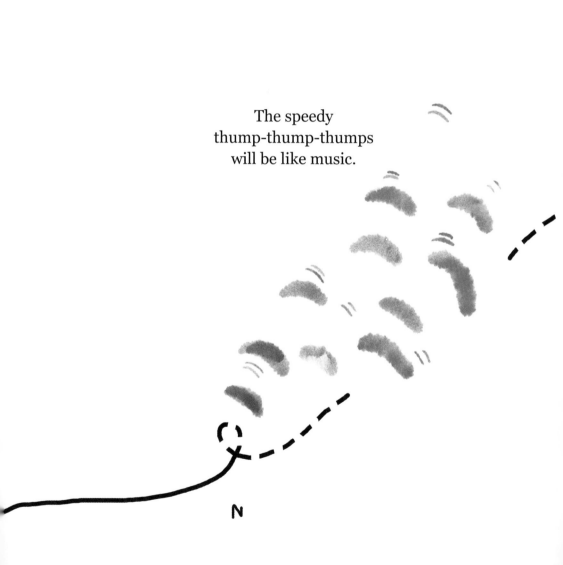

Finally, your baby
will be real.

Finally, you will
be able to relax.

Finally, you will ease into
the sweet future you have
made for yourself.

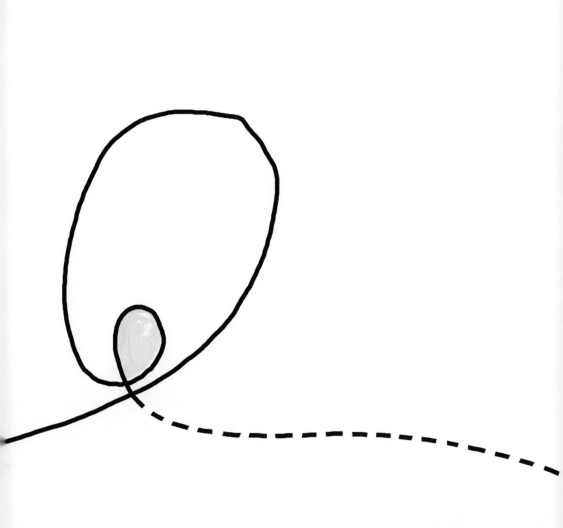

But then—

Silence in the
darkened room.

Searching.

A worried look,
unhelpful questions.

ARE you SUR

LET's WAIT and SE

WE CAN WAIT a FEW

ABOUT YOUR DATES?

WHAT THE DOCTOR SAYS...

AYS and CHECK AGAIN

Something is not right.

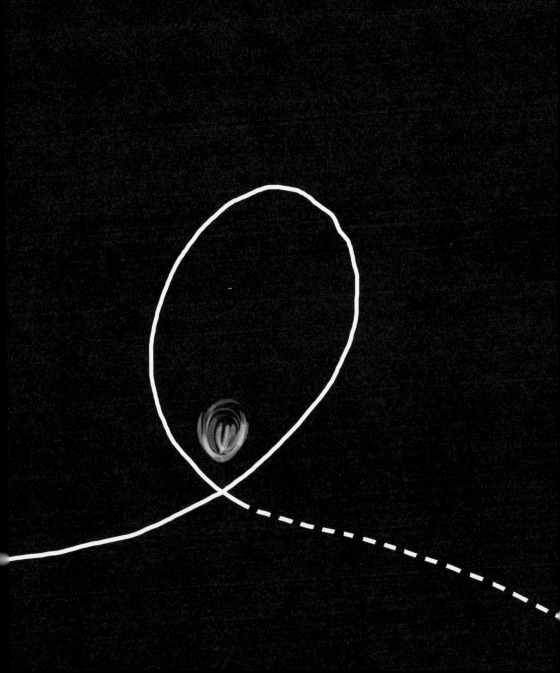

The worst is happening.

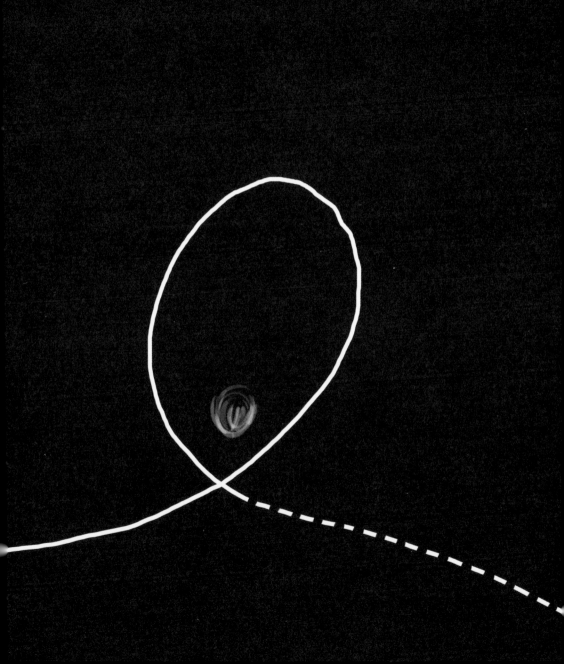

A nightmare, come to life.

They tell you
Your baby is too small.

They tell you
Your baby started growing,
but then stopped.

They tell you
Your baby will need to
go away.

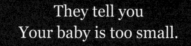

Away.

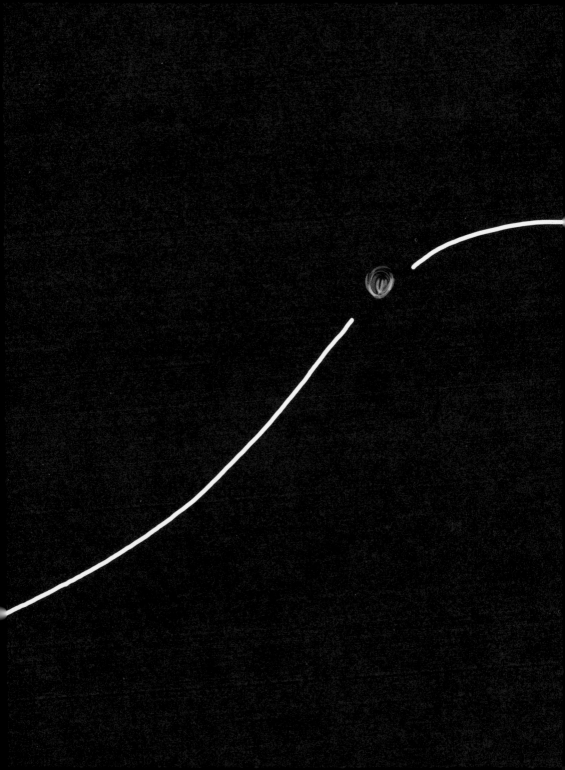

To a place you are not.

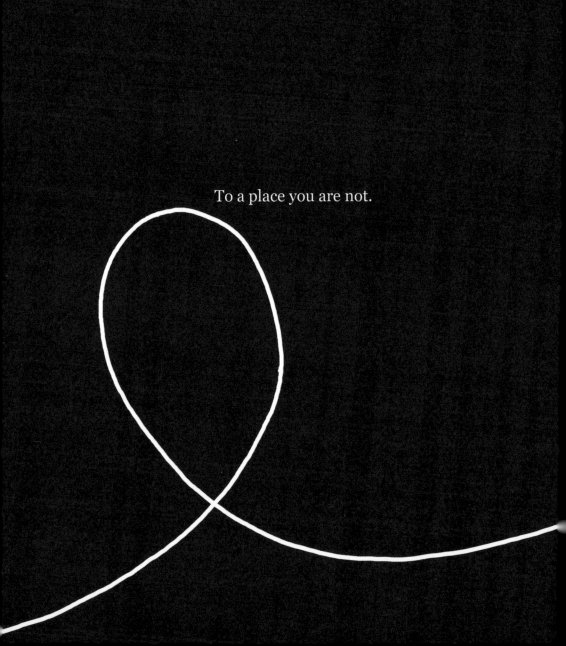

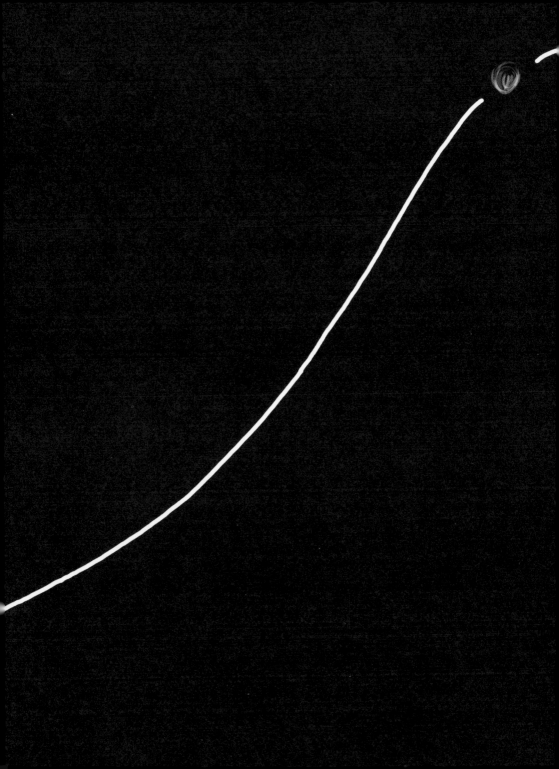

Leaving you behind.

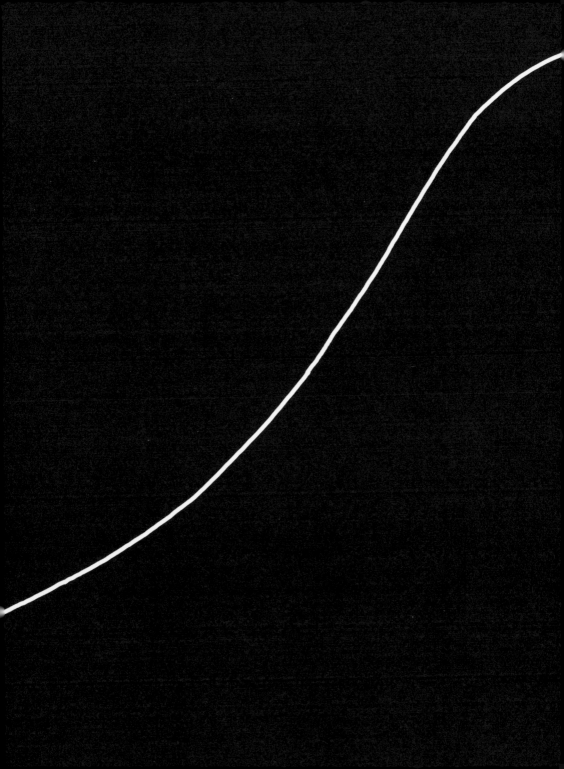

You feel empty
without them.

Alone with
your one and only
heartbeat.

Days pass slowly.

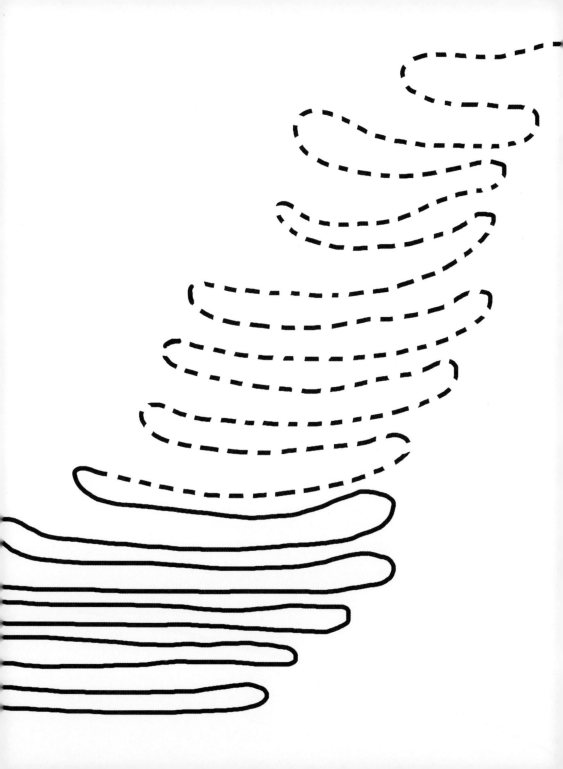

When the sun is out,
you do things you like,
see people you love.

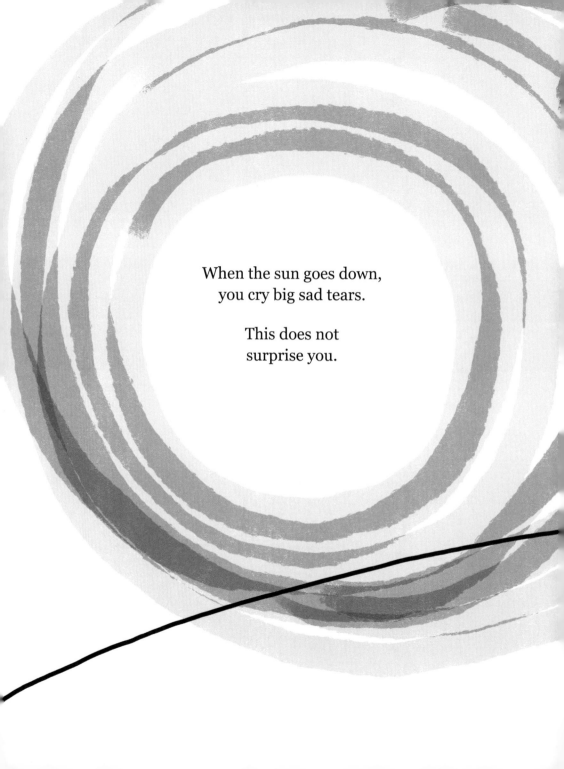

When the sun goes down,
you cry big sad tears.

This does not
surprise you.

You can't stop thinking
that you were right.

This time, something
went wrong.

This future was not
meant to be.

Your best friend reassures you.

Your dad comforts you.

Your partner calms you.

IT WA

you AR

yo

NOT YOUR FAULT

TILL STRONG
and HEALTHY

HAVE TIME

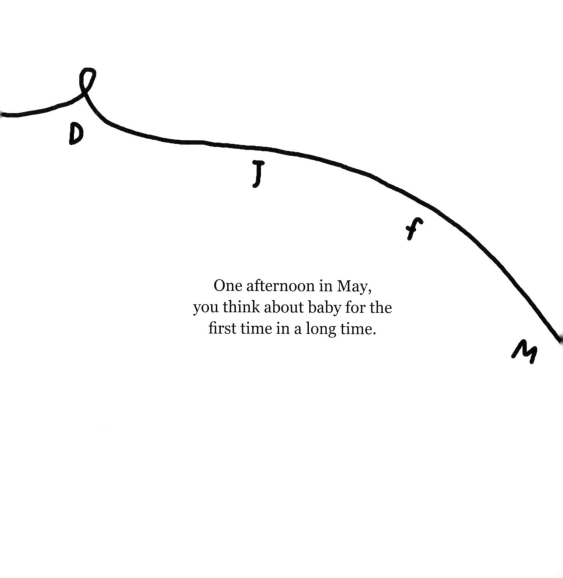

One afternoon in May,
you think about baby for the
first time in a long time.

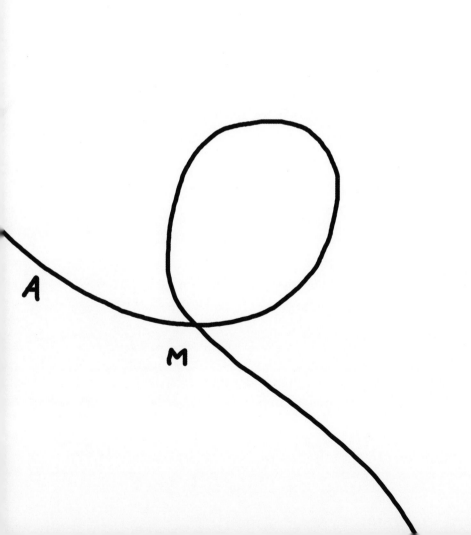

A familiar ache returns.

You sit with it, softly,
until it is ready to go.

The low, gentle hum of
springtime is like music.

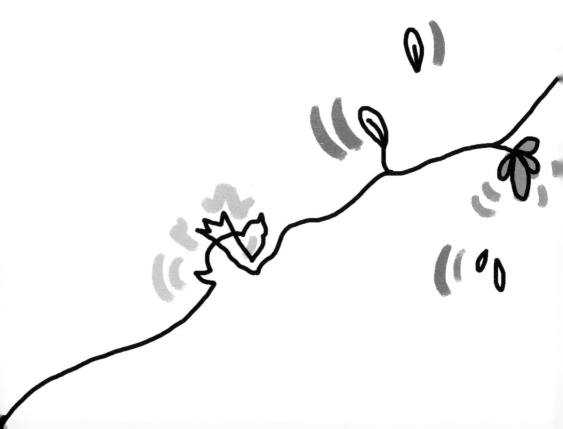

You realize, the world
can be beautiful again.

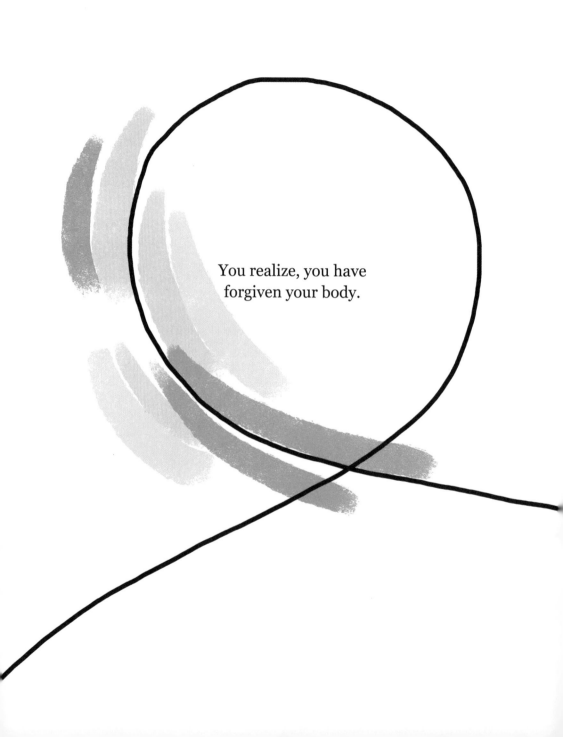

You realize, you have
forgiven your body.

You realize, you can be
friends with your sadness.

This was you.

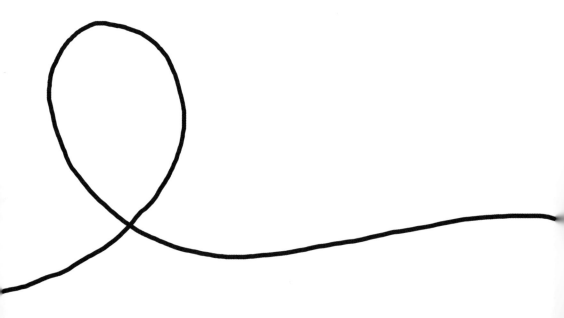

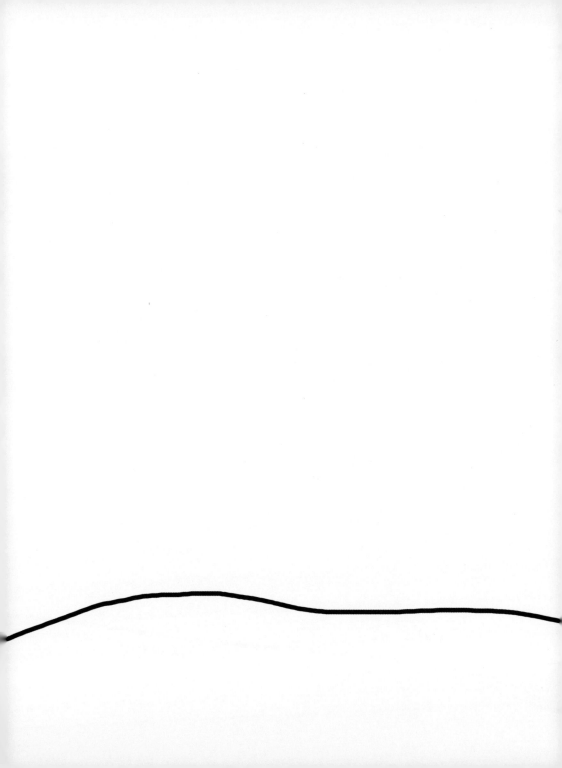

This was you and your baby.

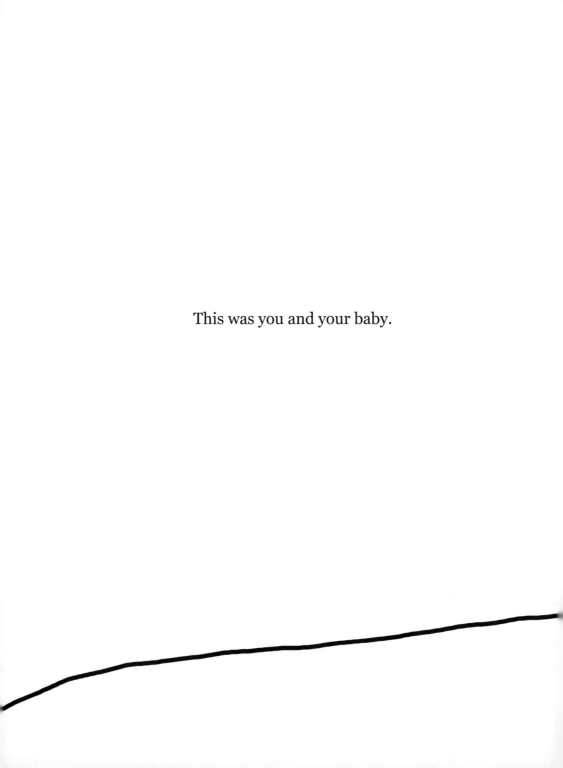

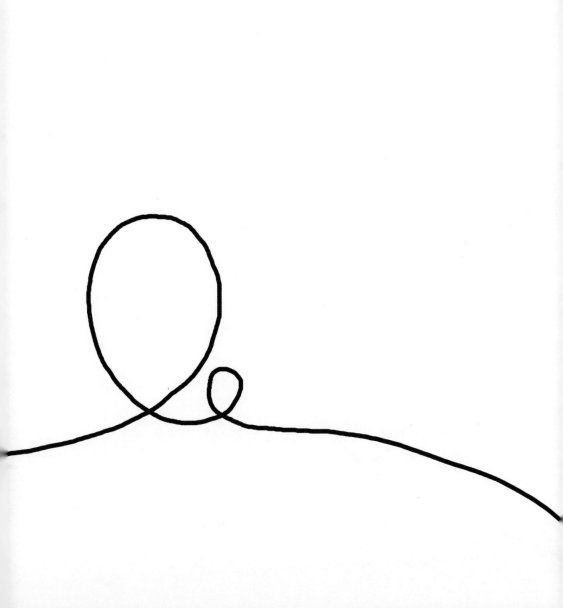

When this was you,
you thought about the
future a lot.

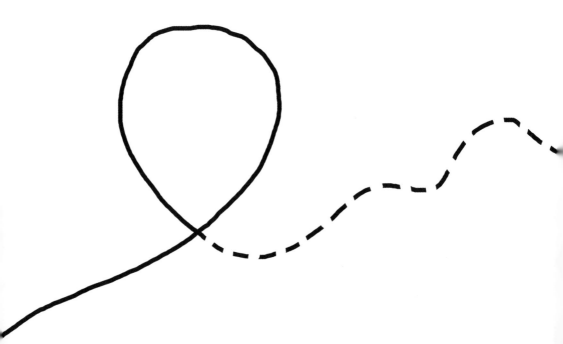

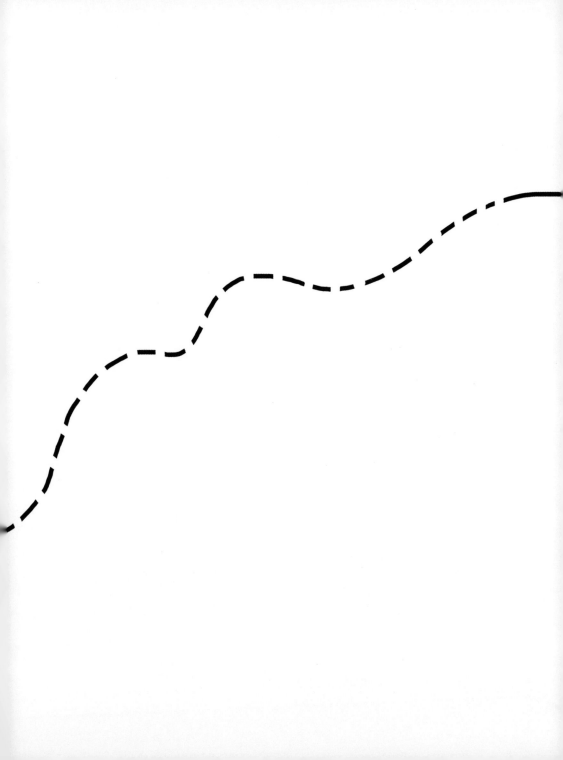

You wondered if you would
be partnered,

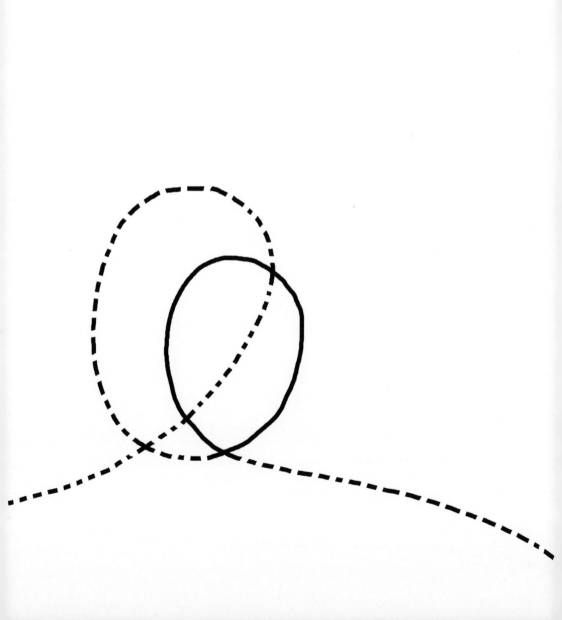

Have a cat,

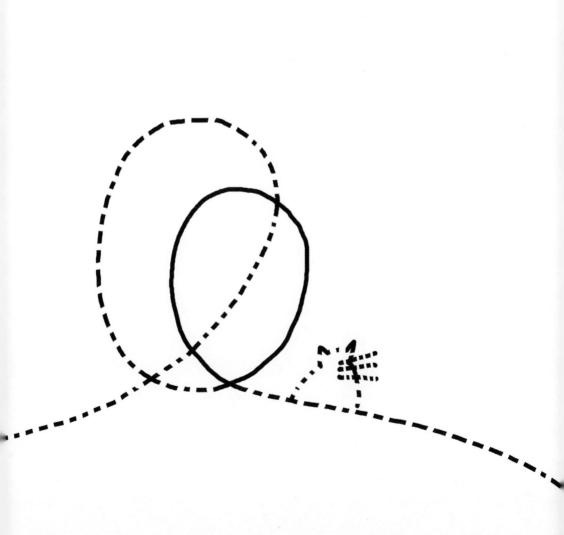

Live in a cozy home.

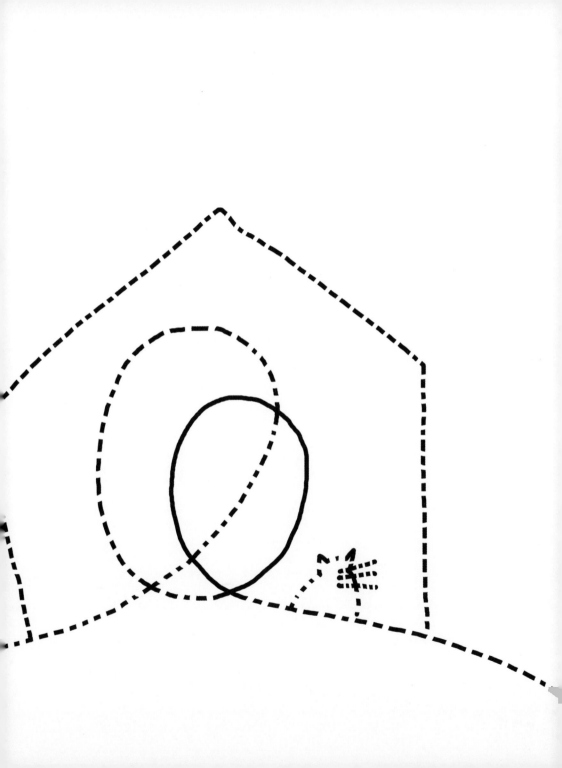

But most of all,
you hoped your future
would include a baby.

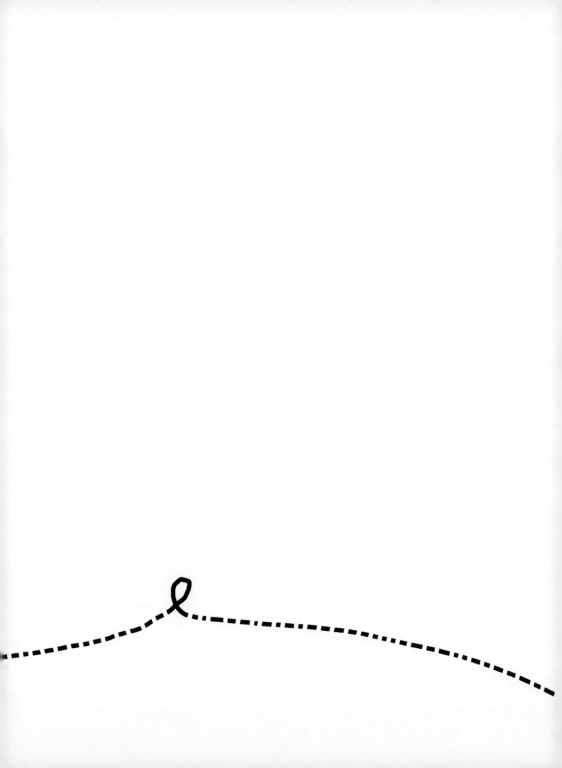

You felt destined to be
a mama and hoped your baby
would find you soon.

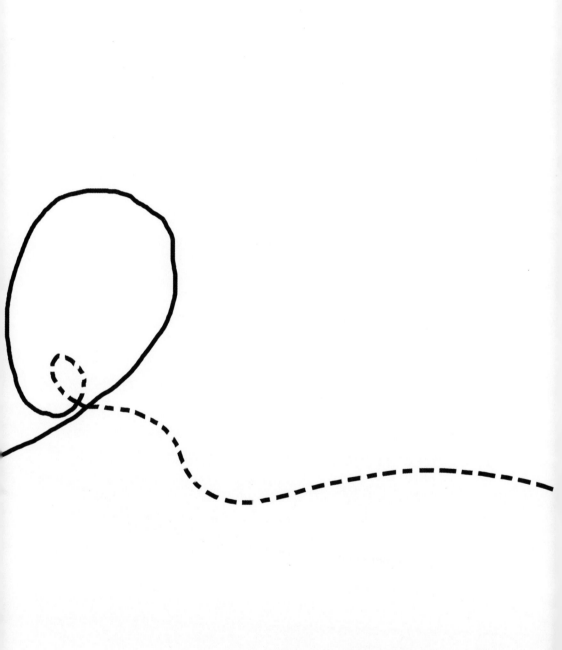

And you still do.

But you wonder about it less
than you did before.

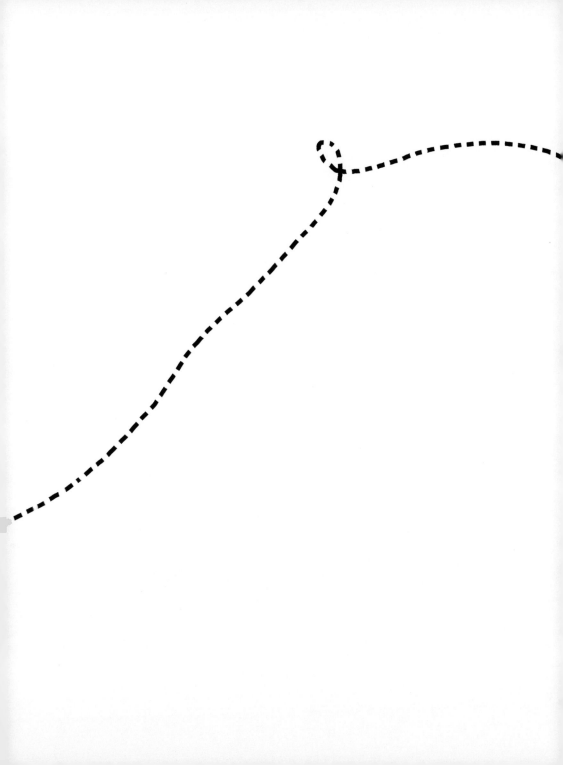

Because you see
the sweet future you have
made for yourself.

One with a partner, a cat,
and a cozy home.

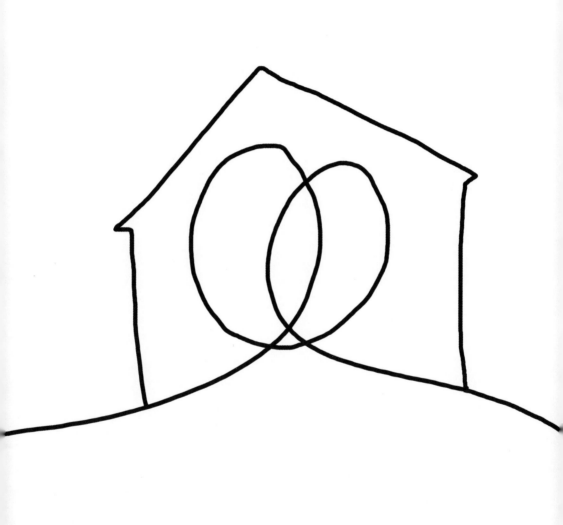

One with friends, travel,
good food and drink.

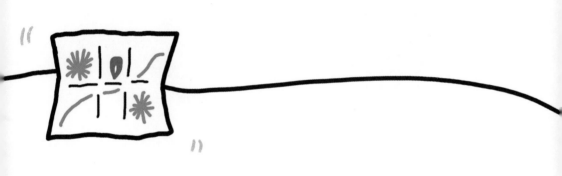

One with love, joy,
and pain all nestled
inside you.

One baby did find you,

Making you a mama forever.

Changing you from
the inside out,

Preparing you for
whatever comes next.

In the meantime,

Enjoy this future.

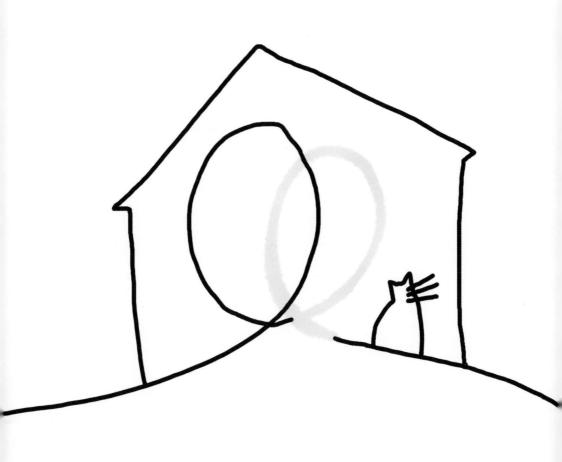

It is surely meant to be.

ABOUT THE AUTHOR

Madeleine Garner is a New York-based writer. Her play, *I Ragazzi*, cowritten with her father, Broadway writer David Goldsmith, was published in 2023 by the Dramatists Play Service and is now available for licensing. Garner was accepted into the Spring 2023 Woodward Residency where she was encouraged to write this book. Garner received her BA in Art History and Italian Studies from Wheaton College in Massachusetts. She resides with her husband, daughter, and cat in Ridgewood.

Madeleine and Giorgia recently published a picture book about the world of data titled, *This Is Me and Only Me*.

ABOUT THE DESIGNER

Giorgia Lupi is an award-winning information designer and partner at Pentagram Design whose work synthesizes data and storytelling in innovative ways to create unique and singular brand expressions. One of the most lauded designers of her generation and a prominent voice in the field of data design, Lupi was the 2022 recipient of the National Design Award from the Cooper Hewitt, Smithsonian Design Museum. Her TED Talk on her humanistic approach to data has over one million views. She has published two books, *Dear Data*, exploring the details of daily life through hand-drawn visual data, and *Observe, Collect, Draw! A Visual Journal*, a guided journal for collecting visual data.

Giorgia and Madeleine recently published a picture book about the world of data titled, *This Is Me and Only Me*.